THE COMP IPHONE 11 SERIES USER GUIDE

The Concise User Guide for Beginners and Seniors to Master your iPhone 11, 11 Pro, 11 Pro Max, IOS 16

Kerry Vinter

THE COMPREHENSIVE
IPHONE 11 SERIES
USER GUIDE

The Concise User Guide for Beginners and Seniors to Master your iPhone 11, 11 Pro, 11 Pro Max, IOS 16

COPYRIGHT PAGE

All rights reserved. No part of this publication may be reproduced, distributed, or transmitted in any form or by any means, including photocopying, recording, or other electronic or mechanical methods, without the publisher's prior written permission.

Copyright © 2022 by Kerry Vinter

Table of Contents

Introduction 6

Turn on and configure iPhone 7

Restart iPhone 10

Update iPhone iOS 11

Restore all content on iPhone from backup ... 14

Restore iPhone from computer backup 15

Switch from Android device to iPhone 17

How to unlock iPhone for use with other media 36

Tips for iPhone 11 39

What is Apple's True Tone display? 42

What is Apple Pay, how does it work and how do you set it up? 48

Keyboard tips 51

Notifications and restrictions 55

Mail tips 61

Maps tips 66

Apple Music tips 68

Safari tips 77

iCloud tips 81

Apple Pay tips 83

Restore iPhone to factory settings 117

Set up a Face ID or add an alternate look 128

Create a password for the new account 132

Browse web pages with Safari on iPhone 136

Conclusion 143

5

Introduction

iPhone has long been the device that makes it super simple to get the basics done. Whether that be sending a text, browsing the web, sharing photos or installing games. But if that's not enough for you and you want to see everything your iPhone has on offer, there's plenty more that you can plunge into head-first. If you've got the iPhone 11, or either the 11 Pro or 11 Pro Max, there's plenty to discover.

Of course, if you have any of the previous or newer few iPhones and you're running iOS 14.6 already, many of these features and tips still apply. So get your cup of tea, sit down and dig through some of these tips, and really get to grips with the latest software on your iPhone.

Turn on and configure iPhone

Turn on and set up your new iPhone online. Your iPhone can also set up by linking it to your computer. If you have an iPhone, iPad, iPod touch, or other Android devices, you can transfer the data to a new iPhone.

For the smoothest possible setting, prepare the following items:

- Connect to the Internet through a Wi-Fi network (you may need a network name and password) or a mobile data service through your service provider.
- Your Apple ID and password; If you do not have an Apple ID, you can create one during setup

- Information about your credit or debit card account if you want to add your card to Apple Pay during setup

Your previous iPhone or backup device if you are transferring data to a new device

Your Android device if you are transmitting Android content

Turn on and set up your iPhone

Press and hold the side button or the Sleep / Wake button (depending on your model) until the Apple logo appears.

If iPhone does not turn on, you may need to charge the battery.

Do one of the following:

- Tap Settings manually, and then follow the on-screen setup instructions.
- If you have another iPhone, iPad or iPod touch running iOS 11, iPadOS 13 or later, you can use the quick start to automatically set up a new device. Pair the two devices, then follow the on-screen instructions to securely copy your many settings, settings, and iCloud keychain. You can then restore the rest of the data and content on the new device using an iCloud backup.
- Or, if both devices have iOS 12.4, iPadOS 13 or later installed, you can transfer all data wirelessly from the old device to the new one. Keep the devices close to each other and connect the power supply until the transfer is complete.

Restarting iPhone

If your iPhone isn't working properly, try restarting it.
Turn the iPhone off and on

To turn off iPhone, do one of the following:

- On an iPhone with a face ID: Press and hold the side button and the volume button at the same time until the sliders appear, and then drag the top slider.
- On iPhone with the Home button: Press and hold the side button or the Sleep / Wake button (depending on your model), and then drag the slider.

All models : Go to Settings> General> Disable, and then drag the slider.

Update iPhone iOS

After upgrading to the latest version of iOS, your data and settings remain the same.

Note. Set up iPhone backup automatically or back up your device manually before upgrading.

Update iPhone automatically

If you didn't turn on auto-update when you first set up iPhone, follow these steps:

Go to Settings> General> Software Update.

Click Configure Automatic Updates (or Automatic Updates). In iOS 13.6 and later, you can automatically download and/or install updates.

When the update becomes available, iPhone will download and install the update overnight when it charges and connects to Wi-Fi. You will receive a notification before installing the update.

Update iPhone manually

You can check for and install software updates at any time. Go to Settings> General> Software Update. The display shows the currently installed version of iOS and whether an update is available. To turn off automatic updates, go to Settings> General> Software Update> Automatic Updates Settings (or Automatic Updates).

Update using your computer

Connect your iPhone to your computer via USB. Do one of the following:

- In the Finder sidebar on your Mac: Choose your iPhone, then tap on General at the upper part of the window.
Note . To use Finder to upgrade your iPhone, you need macOS Catalina. For previous versions of macOS, use iTunes to constantly update your iPhone.
- In iTunes on a Windows PC: Click the iPhone button in the upper-left corner of the iTunes window, and then click Summary.
- Click Check for Updates.

To install the available updates, click the Update button.

Restore all content on iPhone from backup

You can restore content, settings, and applications from a backup to a new or recently removed iPhone.

Restore iPhone from iCloud backup

Turn on a new or recently uninstalled iPhone.

Follow the online instructions to select your language and region.

Click Configure Manually.

Tap Restore from iCloud backup, and then follow the on-screen instructions.

You must provide your Apple ID.

Restore iPhone from computer backup

Use USB to connect your new or removed iPhone to the computer where your backup is located.

Do one of the following:

- In the Finder sidebar on your Mac: Select your iPhone, and then click Trust.
  Note. To use Finder to restore iPhone from backup, you need macOS Catalina. For previous versions of macOS, use iTunes to restore from a backup.
- In iTunes on a Windows PC: If more than one device is connected to the PC, click the device icon at the top left of the iTunes window, and then select a new or recently removed iPhone from the list.

- On the welcome screen, tap Restore from this backup, select your backup from the list, and then click Continue. If your backup is encrypted, you must enter a password before restoring your files and settings.

Switch from Android device to iPhone

When you first set up a new iPhone, you can automatically and securely move data from your Android device.

Follow these steps on your iPhone:

Follow the setup assistant.

- On the Apps & Data screen, tap Move Data from Android.
- On your Android device, follow these steps:
- Turn on wifi.
- Open the Move to iOS app.
- Follow the instructions on the screen.

Manually move content from your Android device to your iPhone, iPad, or iPod touch

Here are some tips for transferring contacts, photos, music, documents, etc. From your Android gadget to your new iPhone iPod touch, or iPad.

The Move to iOS app can also be used to automatically send Android content to your new iPhone, iPod touch, or iPad. If you can't use the program, you can move the content manually.

Mail, contacts, and calendar

The software on your iPhone, iPod touch, or iPad works with email service providers like Google, Yahoo, Microsoft Exchange, etc., so you can save the email, contacts, and calendar you have now. To get started, add each email account to your device. Then go to Settings> Passwords and Accounts. Contact Apple Support for help moving e-mail, contacts, and calendar.

Photos and videos

To transfer photos and videos from your Android device to your iPhone, iPad, or iPod touch, use a computer:

- Connect Android to your computer and find your photos and videos. On most devices, these files can be found in DCIM> Camera. On your Mac, install Android File Transfer, open it, and then go to DCIM> Camera.
- Select the photos and videos you want to move and drag them to a folder on your computer.
- Disconnect Android and connect iPhone, iPad or iPod touch to your computer.
- On a Mac with macOS Catalina, open the Finder. On a Mac with macOS Mojave or earlier, or on a PC, open iTunes. Sync your

photos with your iPhone, iPad or iPod touch on your computer. You can find photos and videos on your device in Photos> Album.
- You can also use iCloud Photos to store your photos and videos in iCloud so you can access your library from any device at any time.

Music

By switching to iPhone, iPad or iPod touch, you can take your music with you. Just use a computer to transfer music. If you're using a music streaming app, go to the App Store, download the app, and sign in with your username and password. If you're using Apple Music, just sign in to your iPhone, iPad or iPod touch.

To transfer music from your Android device to your iPhone, iPad, or iPod touch, use a computer:

- Link your Android gadget to your computer and discover your music. On most devices, these files can be found in the Music section. Install Android File Transfer on your Mac, open it, and then go to Music.
- Select the songs you want to move and drag them to a folder on your computer.
- Disconnect your Android gadget and link your iPhone, iPad, or iPod touch to your PC.
- On a Mac running macOS Mojave 10.14 or later, or on a PC, open iTunes and click Songs.
- Open the folder where you place your songs and drag them to the Songs section of Music or the iTunes library.
- Select your iPhone, iPad or iPod touch and tap Music. You can sync your entire library or select only newly added songs or artists

Click Sync. You can find your music on your iPhone, iPad, or iPod touch in Music.

Books and PDFs

To transfer eBooks from your Android gadget, you can import them to your iPhone, iPod touch, or iPad or access them with apps like Kindle, Nook, Google Play Books, and more. To access books from the app, go to the App Store, download the app, and sign in with your username and password.

To transfer ePub and PDF books from Android to iPhone, iPad or iPod touch, use a computer:

- Link your Android gadget to your computer and discover your books and PDFs. On most devices, these files can be found in

Documents. On your Mac, install Android File Transfer, open it, and then go to Docs.
- Select the books and PDFs you want to move and drag them to a folder on your computer.
- Disconnect your Android device and connect your iPhone to your computer.
- On your Mac, drag books and PDFs into Books. Drag books and PDFs to iTunes on your PC.
- On a Mac with macOS Catalina, open the Finder. On a Mac running macOS Mojave 10.14 or later, or on a PC, open iTunes and sync ePub and PDF books. You can find ePub and PDF books on your iPhone, iPad, or iPod touch from the Books> Library menu.

Documents

If you store the document in the cloud or in another service like Dropbox, Google Drive, or Microsoft OneDrive, you can download the application from the App Store and then log in. You can also bring all the files together with the Files application. Whether your files are on your iPhone, iPad or iPod touch, in iCloud Drive or another service like Dropbox or Box, you can easily browse, search and organize all your files in one place.

Programs for pages, numbers, and major programs work with several types of files, including Microsoft Office documents. If you do not use the cloud to transfer documents, download the programs:

- Move to the App Store on your iPhone, iPad, or iPod touch and have pages installed, Numbers and Keynote.
- Link your Android to your computer and discover your documents. On most devices, these files can be found in Documents. On your Mac, install Android File Transfer, open it, and then go to Docs.
- Select the documents you want to move and drag them to a folder on your computer.
- On a Mac with MacOS Catalina, open the Finder. On a Mac running macOS Mojave 10.14 or later, or on a PC, open iTunes and sync documents from your iPhone, iPad, or iPod touch.

Set up a mobile service

Your mobile phone requires an operator SIM card to connect to your iPhone; Contact your carrier to set up a mobile plan.

Your iPhone can connect to the service provider's network using nano-SIM. On an iPhone that supports dual SIM, you can use nano-SIM and eSIM (not available in all countries or regions). Here are some of the many ways to use a dual SIM card:

- Use one for work and the other for personal calls.
- Add a local rate plan when traveling to another region.
- A separate voice and data plan are available.

Note. To use two different media, you need to unlock your iPhone.

Nano-SIM settings

Insert a paper clip or SIM card remover into the small slot on the SIM card tray, and then tap iPhone to remove the tray. A SIM card clip or tool is inserted into the slot on the right side of the iPhone to press and remove the tray.
Note: The shape and orientation of the SIM card tray depend on your iPhone model and region.

Remove the tray from the iPhone.

Put the nano-SIM in the tray. The angle of inclination determines the correct direction.

Nano-SIM is inserted into the tray on the iPhone; Tilt angle at the top right.

Insert the tray back into the iPhone.

If you have previously set a PIN on the nano-SIM, enter the PIN carefully when prompted.

Set up your mobile rate with eSIM

On models that support eSIM, the operator's eSIM is stored digitally on the iPhone.

Go to Settings> Cellular, and then tap Add Cell Rate.
Position the iPhone so that the QR code provided by your carrier appears in the window, or enter the details manually. You may be asked to enter a verification code provided by your service provider.

Tap Add cellular tariff.

If the new plans are your second line, follow the on-screen instructions to determine how you want the plans to work together.

Besides, you can activate your mobile tariff through the operator application (if supported). Go to the App Store, download the program of your operator, and then use this program to activate the tariff plan. You can store multiple eSIM cards on your iPhone, but you can only use one eSIM card at a time. To switch eSIM, go to Settings> Cellular, tap the plan you want to use, and then tap Enable this line.

Manage your mobile plans

When setting up on dual SIM models, you can choose how your iPhone will use each line. To change the settings later, follow these steps:

Go to Settings> Mobile Phone.
Do the following:

- Tap Cell Data, then select the default bar. To allow iPhone to use any line, depending on coverage and availability, turn on Allow cell data transfer.
- If data roaming is turned on and you are outside the area of your service provider's network, you may be charged for roaming.
- Tap the default voice line, then select a line.
- In Cellular, tap a line, and then change settings, such as Cellular label, Wi-Fi call (if

available from your service provider), Calls to other devices, or SIM card PIN. Tags are displayed in Phones, Messages and Contacts.

When using two SIM cards, note the following:

- For one line, you need to turn on calls over Wi-Fi to allow that line to receive calls while the other line is used for the call. If you receive a call on one line when the other is used for calls, and there is no Wi-Fi connection, iPhone uses the cellular data of the line used for the call to receive a call from the other line. A fee may be charged. The line used for calls should be allowed to use the data in your cellular settings (as the default route or as the default route when Allow cellular data is enabled) to receive calls on another wire.

- If you do not have a Wi-Fi call on the line, all incoming calls on that line (including emergency calls) will be sent directly to voicemail (if available from your service provider) when using another line; You will not receive a notification about missed calls. If you have set up conditional call forwarding (if available from your service provider) from one line to another when the line is busy or not working, calls will not be sent to your voice mail .; Contact your service provider for configuration information.
- If you make a call from another device, such as a Mac, by forwarding it to an iPhone with a dual SIM card, the call will be made using the default voice line.
- If you start an SMS / MMS conversation from one line, you cannot transfer the conversation to another line; You need to

delete chats and start a new one using the other side. In addition, you may incur an additional charge if you send an SMS / MMS attachment over a line that is not selected for mobile data.

Instant Access Point and Personal Access Point use the media selected for mobile data.

Use the SIM card PIN for your iPhone or iPad

Lock the SIM card with a PIN (personal identification number) to request the identification of phone calls and to use mobile data.

To protect your SIM card from others who use it for phone calls or mobile data, you can use the SIM card PIN. Then, every time you restart your device or remove the SIM card, your SIM card is automatically locked and you will see 'SIM locked' in the status bar.

Turn the SIM card PIN on or off

If you have an iPhone, go to Settings> Cellular> SIM PIN. If you have an iPad, go to Settings> Cell Data> SIM PIN.

If prompted, enter the SIM card PIN. If you have never used it, enter the default SIM card PIN from your service provider. If you do not know the default SIM card PIN, do not try to guess it. Check the customer service page of your operator or the documents attached to your tariff plan. Or you can contact your service provider.
Click Finish.

If you forget or do not know your SIM card PIN

34

Never try to guess your SIM PIN or PUK code. * An incorrect guess can lock your SIM card forever, and then you will need a new one. If your device asks for a PIN or a code without your knowledge, here's what to do:

Contact your service provider who has provided you with a SIM card. If you are not sure which operator to call, remove the SIM card and check the operator's name or logo. Ask your service provider to help you unlock your SIM card with the default PIN or PUK code. If you cannot unlock the SIM card using the SIM PIN or PUK code, or if the message says 'PUK is out of place', ask for a new SIM card.

How to unlock iPhone for use with other media

Unlocking your iPhone means you can use it with a variety of media. Your iPhone may be blocked by an operator. Unlocking your iPhone means you can use it with a variety of media. Follow these steps to contact your carrier and unlock your iPhone.

Only your operator can unlock your iPhone. Contact your operator and ask to unlock. Your account may need to be unlocked. It may take a few days after you submit your request. To check the status of your unlock request, contact your carrier.

After the operator confirms that they have unlocked your iPhone, follow these steps:

- If you have a SIM card from a service provider other than your current one

To unlock iPhone, follow these steps:

- Remove the SIM card.
- Insert a new SIM card. Your device is activated.
- If you do not have another SIM card to use

To unlock iPhone, follow these steps:

- Back up your iPhone.
- After backing up, delete iPhone.
- Restore iPhone from the backup you just created.
- Connect your iPhone to the Internet
- Connect iPhone to the Internet using Wi-Fi or available cellular networks.

Connect iPhone to Wi-Fi

Go to Settings> Wi-Fi, then turn on Wi-Fi.

Touch one of the following options:

- One network: enter a password if required.
- Other: Join a hidden network. Enter the name of the hidden network, security type and password.
- If the Wi-Fi icon appears at the top of the screen, iPhone is connected to a Wi-Fi network. (To check this, open Safari to browse the web.) The iPhone will reconnect when you return to your original location.
- Join a personal access point
- If your iPad (Wi-Fi + cellular) or other iPhone uses a personal access point, you can use its mobile Internet connection. Go to Settings> Wi-Fi as well

Tips for iPhone 11

Home screen and display

Rearrange home screen icons: Now that there's no more pressure sensitive display, some of the long press and force touch actions have changed. There are two ways to rearrange your app icons. Either long press on an app and tap "rearrange apps" in the pop up menu, or just long press and drag the icon before the pop up menu has even appeared.

Enable dark mode: Go to Settings > Display & Brightness and now toggle on the Dark Mode. You can also get it to automatically change based on time or sunrise/sunset.

Get wallpapers to darken with Dark Mode: With a few of the reinstalled wallpapers, you can get the image to darken and change whenever dark mode is enabled. Go to Settings > Wallpaper and make sue the "dark appearance dims wallpaper" toggle is switched on. Then hit "choose new wallpaper" and pick one from "Stills" or "Live" which has the little eclipse icon in the bottom right corner. Now, whenever dark mode is enabled, the wallpaper will also go dark.

Quickly add multiple apps to a folder: This one's been around for a couple of years, but rather than just individually, slowly dragging one app at a time into a folder, you can bunch them together quickly. Long press an app and drag it on top of another icon, then quickly tap any other apps to form a floating group of apps.

Standard or Zoomed display: Since iPhone 6 Plus you've been able to choose between two resolution options. You can change the display setting from Standard or Zoomed. To switch between the two - if you've changed your mind after setup - go to Settings > Display & Brightness > Display Zoom and select Standard or Zoomed.

Set the screen brightness: Either bring up Control Centre - by swiping down from the top right corner of the screen - and adjust the display brightness slider, or go to Settings > Display & Brightness.

Enable True Tone display: To get the iPhone's screen to automatically adjust its colour balance and temperature to match the ambient light in the room, head to Control Centre and long press the screen brightness slider. Now tap the True Tone button. You can also go to Settings > Display and Brightness and toggle the "True Tone" switch.

What is Apple's True Tone display?

Text Size and Bold Text: To change the default text size, go to Settings > Display & Brightness, then choose the "Text Size" option before adjusting the slider to change the size. Beneath "Text Size" you'll also find a toggle for bold text, switch it on if you find the standard fine text too difficult to read.

Night Shift: As well as True Tone, there's an option called Night Shift that cuts out blue light helping your eyes to relax. Bring up Control Centre, then long press the display brightness slider and select the Night Shift button.

Choose a new wallpaper: As with all new iPhones, Apple has completely revamped its wallpaper offering for the new models. New wallpapers to be had in the Settings > Wallpaper. Here you'll find a refreshed selection of both Dynamic and Live wallpapers.

Crop and markup screenshots: Take a screenshot, then a small preview screenshot appears in the bottom left corner. Tap it and then use the tools shown to draw, write on, or crop the image.

Dismiss screenshot preview: To get the little screenshot preview off your screen, just swipe it left. Hey presto! It's gone.

Get to Wi-Fi settings quickly: Long press on the Settings icon to reveal quick links to Battery, Mobile Data, Wi-Fi and Bluetooth settings. The move makes it really speedy to jump to the wireless settings.

Buttons, gestures and controls

Drag the scroll bar: You might notice that when you're scrolling through lists or apps, a subtle slim bar appears on the right side. If you long press on it, it'll get thicker, and then you can drag that up and down to quickly scroll.

Quickly toggle dark mode: Open up Control Centre by dragging it down from the top of the screen, then long press on the screen brightness slider. Here you'll find a new dark mode toggle alongside the usual True Tone and auto-brightness options.

Quickly view available Wi-Fi networks: In a similar move to the above, you can see what Wi-Fi networks are available by dragging down Control Centre and then long pressing on the Wi-Fi icon.

Switch between apps, fast: If you want to quickly switch between apps, just drag from left to right on the bottom of the screen where the bar normally appears. This will launch the previous app you were in, and you can keep going back by continuing to swipe.

Take a screenshot: If you had an iPhone X or XS before you'll already know this, but for those moving from older phones you'll need to learn a new way to snap screenshots. Simply press the power button and the volume up button together quickly and it'll snap a screenshot of whatever is on the screen.

Go Home: No, not literally, we're not that rude. Whenever you want to go back to your home screen from an app, just quickly swipe up from the bottom of the screen where you'll see a slim white bar.

Launch recent apps/multitasking screen: Swipe up from the bottom of the screen and then hold your finger in the middle of the screen for a second or two, and now you'll see the familiar screen with app thumbnail cards.

Unlock your phone: Presuming you've registered your face data with Face ID, you can unlock your phone by simply picking up your phone while looking at it and swiping up from the bottom of the screen.

Launch Siri: While you can use the "Hey Siri" hot word to wake up Apple's digital assistant, there's still a way to launch the function using a button press. Press and hold the wake/sleep button on the right side of the phone until the Siri interface pops up on screen.

Switch your phone off: Because long-pressing the wake/sleep button launches Siri now, there's a new method for switching the phone off. To do so, you need to press and hold the wake/sleep button and the volume down button at the same time. Now slide to power off.

What is Apple Pay, how does it work and how do you set it up?

Launch Apple Pay: Again, the wake/sleep button is the key here. Double click it and it'll bring up your Apple Wallet, then scan your face and it will ask you to hold your phone close to the payment machine.

Camera and Photos

Quickly capture video: One cool interface in the camera app is the ability to quickly shoot a video within the Photo mode. All you have to do is drag the shutter button towards the camera switcher and it'll automatically switch to video and start recording once you let go.

Quick burst of photos: In a similar move to the quick video capture, you can drag the shutter towards the camera roll to quickly grab a burst of photos.

Switch between wide, ultra-wide and zoom: To quickly switch between the two or three cameras on the back of your iPhone, just tap the little "1x" icon on the screen. If you'd rather zoom more smoothly, you can just swipe up or down the screen and watch as the zoom scroll-wheel moves.

Take a Slofie: Smartphones have been able to take slow motion videos for some time, but with the iPhone 11, Apple has enabled it from the front facing camera. To take a so-called Slofie, switch to the Slow Mo option in the camera app and just tap the camera switcher icon to switch to the front camera. Press record and you'll have a slow motion selfie video.

Quick access to settings: When you're shooting a photo you might want to quickly get to your settings toggles. All you have to do is swipe up above the shutter button and you'll get a row of options including switching the flash on, changing the aspect ratio, enabling live photos, setting a timer or choosing a live filter.

Keyboard tips

Swipe to type: One features is the ability to type on the keyboard by just swiping across the letters. Start off on the first letter of the word, and just swipe through the others in order to type quickly. When you need a double letter in the middle of the word, just hold that letter for a short while before continuing through the swiping motion.

Go one-handed: QuickType keyboard lets you type one-handed, which is great on the bigger devices like the iPhone 11 Pro Max. Press and hold the globe icon and select either the left or right sided keyboard. It shrinks the keyboard and moves it to one side of the display. Go back to full size by tapping the little arrow.

Use your keyboard as a trackpad: Now that 3D Touch is officially dead, you can no longer use the trackpad feature by pressing hard on the keyboard. Instead, now you need to long-press on the space bar, and it'll launch the same function, now swipe around the keypad to move the cursor around.

Picking your Emoji colour: For the past few years, Emoji have had the option to change skin tone. To access them, go to the emoji keyboard by tapping the globe icon, then long press on the emoji you want to use. If it has alternative skin colour options they will show.

Adding third party keyboards: Install the app (SwiftKey or Gboard are good examples) and follow the instructions in the app. At some point it will ask you to go to Settings > General > Keyboard > Keyboards and add the third-party keyboard.

Accessing additional keyboards beyond Emoji: If you have more multiple keyboards installed, long-press the globe icon on the keyboard and you'll get a pop-up list showing you the options you can use. Tapping the globe icon lets you switch quickly to the next keyboard.

Disable keyboard capitalisation: Until iOS 9, whether you touched the shift key or not, all the letters on the keyboard were capitalised. Now, the keyboard shows the letters in lower case when the shift is off. But if you don't want this, you can disable it by going to Settings > Accessibility > Keyboard and toggling off the "Show Lowercase Keys" option.

Disable keyboard animations: Apple's keyboard has a pop-up character animation that serves as feedback when you tap the keys. You can shut it off

(Settings > General > Keyboard > Character Preview).

Text replacement shortcuts: As in all previous years, one of iOS' most useful keyboard solutions is creating short-codes that turn into full words or phrases. Go to Settings > General > Keyboard > Text Replacement. We find it useful to have one for an address that fills in automatically whenever we misspell "address", adding an extra "s" at the end.

Notifications and restrictions

Expand your notification clusters: By default iOS clusters multiple notifications from the same app in a little virtual pile on your lock screen. To expand them and see all of the individual notifications in a list, just tap on the pile.

Deliver notifications quietly: One interesting new notification management tool lets you send notifications from specific apps to Notification Centre without alerting you with a sound, app badge or lighting up your lock screen. If you want to use this feature, swipe left on a notification (or group of notifications from a specific app) and hit the "manage" option. Now choose "Deliver Quietly".

Turn off notifications from an app: Same method as the "Deliver Quietly" feature, except you tap the "Turn off." option.

Schedule Downtime: Head to Settings > Screentime and choose the Downtime option. Toggle the switch to the "on" position and choose to schedule a time when only specific apps and phone calls are allowed.

Set app limits: Next in the Screentime menu is App Limits. Choose this option and press "add limit" before choosing which category of apps you want to add a time limit to. Select the category and then "add" before choosing a time limit and hitting "set".

Choose "always allowed" apps: By default, iOS organises apps into various categories which is both very convenient and inconvenient. For instance,

WhatsApp and Facebook Messenger are lumped in with social networking apps. So if they're your primary communication apps, you'll want to make sure there's no limit on them.

In the main Screentime settings menu, tap "Always Allowed" and manually select the apps you want to ensure aren't impacted by the time limits you've set.

Content & Privacy restrictions: This section is also within the main Screentime settings menu and particularly useful if you're a parent with kids who use iOS devices. Using it you can restrict all manner of content and options, including iTunes and in-app purchases, location services, advertising and so on. It's worth taking a look at.

Limit content access: As part of the content/privacy restrictions, choose the "Content restrictions" option and here you can limit inappropriate content access including TV shows, websites, books, audio and more.

Notes tips

Quickly create a checklist: Long press on the Notes app icon and choose "New Checklist" and then start creating your checklist immediately.

How to share and collaborate on notes: There's a new share icon within Notes that looks like the silhouette of a person and a "+" icon next to it. Tap it, and you can add contacts who can view or make changes in real time.

Turning on passwords in Notes: To password protect individual notes go to Settings > Notes >

Password. Here you can set a default password for all your notes, and you can enable Face ID too.

Lock a note: Open Notes, then long press on one of the notes in your list. Tap "Lock Note" in the drop down menu. Now type in your password, and it'll be locked. You can also do it by opening a note, then pressing the share icon and then the "Lock Note" icon. That merely adds the lock icon to the Note. Complicated we know.

Now tap on the icon to lock the Note. Next time you access it you will need the password. Be warned if you are trying to access it on a iOS device you've not updated to 9.3 or later you won't be able to access it on that device.

Handwritten Notes: Open the Notes app, then tap the new note icon in the bottom right, and select the pen tool above the keyboard. Now scribble away until your heart's content.

Save attachments to Notes: The system-wide Share button has added support for Notes. So, when in Safari, for instance, tap the Share button to save attachments, such as a link or document, to a new or existing note. There's also an Attachments browser in Notes that organises attachments in a single view (tap the grid icon in the lower-left corner).

Mail tips

How to check unread emails in Mail: Go to any of your inboxes in the Mail app and tap the small circle icon with three bars in it decreasing in size. Now it will show you only your unread messages.

How to reply to a specific email in a threaded message: There's a threaded Mail feature in iOS Mail that allows you to reply to messages within the thread rather than just the latest one. Go to a conversation thread and then swipe left on an individual message to reveal a reply button, a flag button and a delete button.

How to have multiple emails on the go at once: You can now have multiple emails on the go at once, handy if you are in the middle of replying to someone and then have to send a quick email in between.

On an open email that is being composed drag down from the subject line to dock the email. You can keep doing this. When you want to access one of those emails, or see what you've got open, drag the one on top down further and you'll get a view of all of the emails you are working on. To close them, swipe to the right.

Mark as Read: In your inbox swipe from left to right to reveal a "Read" icon. If it's a conversation you will have to do this for as any time as there are unread messages.

More, Flag, Trash: Swiping from right to left reveals quick actions to let you do a number of things. "More" brings up a secondary menu to let you reply, forward, flag, mark as unread, move to junk, or notify you of future messages in this conversation while Flag and Trash let you do just that.

Quick delete/archive: Swipe left on any email in your inbox, and continue swiping until you've made it the whole way across the screen.

Changing the swipe options: You can also change what happens when you swipe left or right in Settings. Go Settings > Mail > Swipe Options and then set your Swipe Left command and your Swipe Right command. Options are limited, but it is something.

Reply notifications: If you are waiting for a specific response from an email and don't want to have to keep checking your phone every two minutes, you can opt for your device to notify you. Swipe from right to left, then tap "More" and select "Notify me" from the list.

Build out your contacts book: When you get a mail from someone and they've got a signature, Apple now reads that information and asks you whether you want to add it to a contact. If you don't want to, you can choose to ignore, but if you do, press on the Add to Contacts button at the top of the screen.

Search: Drag down in your inbox to reveal a search box. You can now search your entire inbox for a keyword rather than just To, From, Subject. You can also limit your search to All mailboxes or the current mailbox you are in. Furthermore, you can also limit it to conversation threads.

Mark all as read: You can now mark all as read in Mail. Yay. In a mailbox, or the combined inbox, you just tap "Edit" at the upper right, then tap "Select All" at the top left. Then choose "Mark" in the bottom corner and choose "Mark as read" from the pop-up menu and all your messages should be marked as read.

Use Mail Drop on iOS: Mail Drop was introduced in Mac OS X to let you easily send large email attachments via iCloud. That same feature is available in the iOS Mail app, letting you attach a large file (5GB to 20GB). When you attach the file, you'll see a popup window with the option to use Mail Drop. Simples.

Maps tips

3D buildings in Maps: Apple has added new 3D buildings within its Street View alternative in Maps, but it's limited to specific cities and locations. Head to San Francisco or New York in the Maps app and tap the new binoculars icon in the app to see a Street View-like view.

How to set preferred transport type in Apple Maps: If you find you only ever use Apple Maps when walking you can set the preferred transport type to be just that. To change it between Driving, Walking, and Public Transport go to Settings > Maps and pick the one you want.

Us ARKit in FlyOver: A few years ago, Apple developed its own Maps app, complete with Flyover; virtual 3D versions of major cities. Now you can look around 3D cities just by moving your iPhone. Search for a major city - like London or New York - then tap the "FlyOver" option. Then all you need to do is move your device and look around the city.

Use indoor maps: For the first time in Apple Maps, iOS 11 enabled indoor mapping to find your way around major malls. It's slowly grown since then, and you can try it in in a whole host of popular international airports. To use indoor maps, just search for a supported location and pinch-to-zoom in until the outdoor areas go dark grey. Now you can see inside the building.

Move between building levels on indoor maps: Once you're inside a building map, you'll see a number in the right side of the screen. Tap it, and then choose a floor level.

Apple Music tips

How to hide Apple Music: You have been able to completely hide Apple's Apple Music since iOS 12. To do so, go to Settings > Music and then toggle off "Show Apple Music". Now when you go to the app you will only see your music, rather than the music available on the service.

How to access your entire music library: To see all the songs, albums, and playlists that you added from the Apple Music catalogue, as well as any music that you bought from iTunes, including CDs that you ripped, simply tap the Library tab from the app's menu bar along the bottom.

How to edit your Library categories: To clean up your library and specify which categories you'd like to see at a glance, such as genres, artists, or song, tap the Edit button in the top right of the Library screen, and then toggle on/off your preferences.

How to find your downloaded music: If you only want to see the music that's physically on your device, tap the Library tab from the app's menu bar along the bottom, and then tap Downloaded Music.

How to create a new playlist: Going on a road trip and want to make a playlist? Easy. Tap the Library tab from the app's menu bar along the bottom, then tap Playlists, and select New Playlist. From there, you can add a playlist name, description, music, and toggle on/off whether you want the playlist public.

How to find Apple's curated playlists: The "Listen Now" tab found in the menu bar along the bottom is a place where you can go to in order to find music suggestions hand-selected by the Apple Music team. Suggestions include a curated favorite mix, daily playlists, artist spotlights, and new releases, all of which target you and are tailored to your music preferences.

How to search in Apple Music: Tap the Search icon in the menu bar along the bottom in order to access a dedicated search field, where you can manually type-in artists' names, album titles, etc. You can even search using lyrics from the song if you've forgotten the name of the song or the artist.

How to find top music charts: Go to the Browse tab in the menu bar along the bottom, and then tap "Top Charts" to see a regularly updated list of the most popular songs on Apple Music.

How to find top music charts by genre: By default, the Top Charts section in the Browse tab shows you all genres. But you can choose a specific genre, such as Blues, by scrolling down until you see a "More to Explore" section.

How to find videos: Apple Music isn't just about music. It's also about music videos and other video content. Go to the Browse tab in the menu bar along the bottom, and scroll down until you see Apple Music TV.

How to share an album: Want to share an album via Twitter, Facebook, or wherever? Tap on any album, and then select the button with the (...) three dots at the top. From there, tap Share Album and select how you'd like to share it.

How to add an album to your Play Next queue: Apple Music can queue up albums you want to listen to while on the go. Just add it to your Play

Next list. Tap on any album, and then select the button with the (...) three dots at the top. From there, tap "Play Next".

How to add an album to a playlist: You can add an entire album to a new or old playlist. Just tap on the album, and then select the button with the (...) three dots at the top. From there, tap "Add to a Playlist", and then select which playlist (old or new) you want to add it to.

How to download an album to your Library for offline listening: Tap on the album, and then select the button with the (...) three dots at the top. From there, tap Add to a Library. You will then be brought back to the album screen. Now just tap the icon that looks like a cloud with a downward pointing arrow.

How to love/dislike an album: You can tell Apple Music if you love or dislike an album so that it can better tailor music suggestions to you. Tap on any album, and then select the button with the (...) three dots. From there, tap Love or Dislike, depending on your preference.

How to create a station from a song: Tap on any song, and then from the music controls menu (tap it along the bottom to make it expand into a full screen card) select the button with the (...) three dots in the lower corner. From there, tap Create Station. This will create a radio station based on that specific song.

How to share a song: Want to share an album via Twitter, Facebook, or wherever? Tap on any song, and then from the music controls menu (tap it along the bottom to make it expand into a full screen card) select the button with the (...) three dots in the lower corner. From there, tap Share Album, and then click how you'd like to share.

How to add a song to your Play Next queue: Apple Music can queue up songs you want to listen to while on the go. Just add it to your Play Next list. Tap on any song, and then from the music controls menu (tap it along the bottom to make it expand into a full screen card) select the button with the (...) three dots in the lower corner. From there, tap "Play Next".

How to add a song to a playlist: Tap on any song, and then from the music controls menu (tap it along the bottom to make it expand into a full screen card) select the button with the (...) three dots in the lower corner. From there, tap Add to a Playlist, and then select which playlist (old or new).

How to download a song to your Library for offline listening: Tap on any song, and then add them to your library by tapping the little "+" icon, then hit the cloud download icon.

How to see lyrics for a song: Can't tell what the artist in a song is saying? Check out the lyrics in Apple Music. Tap on any song, and then from the music controls menu (tap it along the bottom to make it expand into a full screen card) select the button that looks like a speech bubble with quotation marks inside it.

Share an artist: Like songs and albums, you can share an artist with a friend via social networks and messaging apps. Just tap on any artist's page (search for an artist, then click his or her name to access the page, etc.), then tap the button with the (...) three dots next to their name, and select Share Artist. From there, pick how you'd like to share.

Safari tips

Stop websites tracking you: Go to Settings > Safari and then toggle the "Prevent cross-site tracking" switch to the on position.

Access saved passwords: Thanks to iCloud, Safari has the ability to store your password across all your devices. Go to Settings > Passwords & Accounts > Website & App Passwords then log in using your Face ID scanner. Here you can see all the passwords that are saved, and manage them.

Find on Page in Safari: To Find text in a Safari page, hit the Share button on a page to see a Find on Page option (it surfaces a pop-up over the keyboard).

Disable frequently-visited sites in Safari: Safari displays icons of your most visited websites every time you open a new page. It lets you delete individual ones by tapping and holding on them, but now you can turn them off entirely by going to Settings > Safari. From there, turn off Frequently Visited Sites.

DuckDuckGo: If you want to set DuckDuckGo as your default search engine over Google, Yahoo, or Bing, go to Settings > Safari > Search Engine and select the private friendly search engine as the default.

Auto suggesting websites: Like Safari on the desktop you can have the iPhone or iPad Safari recommend suggested search results as you type. It's on as default but if you don't want it, go to Settings > Safari > Search Engine Suggestions and toggle the feature off.

Auto suggesting apps: Likewise as you type in popular app names into the Safari search URL box, Apple will try and match that with apps you either have or might want. It's on as default, but if you want to turn if off go to Settings > Safari > Safari Suggestions.

Making websites load faster or saving your data: Safari preloads the first hit of the search result to make loading your choice seem quicker. The downside is that this could use up data. If you want to turn it off go to Settings > Safari > Preload Top Hit and turn it off.

Scan your credit card: Rather than having to type all your details you can now use the camera to scan your credit card. When it comes to entering the credit card details either press to auto fill if you are already using that feature with Keychain, or press it and then select Use Camera on the next menu you get.

Swipe forwards and backwards: Swiping from off the screen on to the screen from the left of the screen goes back through your browsing history while swiping from the right of Safari goes forward through your browsing history.

iCloud tips

Find your devices (and friends): Find my Friends has gone, but that doesn't mean you can't find them anymore. Apple just moved all the location tracking services in to one Find My app. Just open it up and you'll see a tab for contacts and another for devices. It's simple.

Turn on iCloud Drive: Go to Settings, tap on your name/ID at the top then go to iCloud > iCloud Drive. Toggle it on or off.

Manage your Storage: Settings, then your name/ID > iCloud > Manage Storage. From here you can see how much storage you have, how much you have left, and choose to buy more.

Family Sharing: Rather than have your iTunes account on all your family's iPhones and iPads you can now set up Family Sharing for up to 5 people. Go to Settings then tap your name/ID at the top and choose the "Family Sharing" option.

Secure iCloud Keychain Access: Go to Settings, then your name/ID at the top > iCloud > Keychain, and toggle it on or off.

Access iCloud Drive files: iOS 11 introduced Files app in 2017. Find it, then tap "Browse" tab and you'll see all of the files and folders in your account.

Apple Pay tips

How to allow Apple Pay Payments on Mac: You can use Apple Pay on your iPhone to confirm payments on a nearby Mac. To ensure this is turned on go to Settings > Wallet & Apple Pay and turn on "Allow Payments on Mac".

How to change the default Apple Pay card: Go to Settings > Wallet & Apple Pay and select the Default Card you want. If you only have one card it will automatically be the default card.

Take a photo

Photo is the standard mode you see when you open the Camera. Use photo mode to take photos. Swipe left or right to select another mode, such as Video, Panorama, Slow Motion, Slo-mo, and Portrait.

Tap the home screen or swipe to the left of the lock screen to open the camera in photo mode.

Press the shutter button or any volume button to shoot.

Turn the flash on or off

Press the flash button, and then select Auto, On, or Off.

On iPhone SE (2nd generation), iPhone 11, iPhone 11 Pro, and iPhone 11 Pro Max press the flash button to turn the flash on or off. Or, tap the camera control button, and then press the flash button below the frame to select Auto, On, or Off.

Timer

Compose your shots and stabilize your iPhone, then press the timer button at the top of the screen.

On iPhone SE (2nd generation), iPhone 11, iPhone 11 Pro, and iPhone 11 Pro Max, press the camera control button and then the Timer button.

Zoom in or out

On all models, click on Camera and to zoom in or out pinch the screen.

On iPhone XS, iPhone XS Max, iPhone X, iPhone 8 Plus, and iPhone 7 Plus, switch between 1x or 2x to zoom. To zoom in more than twice, tap and hold the zoom controller and drag the slider to the left. On iPhone 11, switch between 1x or 0.5x to zoom out. To zoom in more than twice, tap and hold the zoom controller and drag the slider to the left.

If you are using iPhone 11 Pro and iPhone 11 Pro Max, click 2 to zoom in and to zoom out tap .5. To zoom in more than twice, tap and hold the zoom controller and drag the slider to the left.

Adjust the focus and exposure of the camera

If you want to snap a photo, the iPhone camera will automatically maintain the focus and exposure, and face recognition balances the exposure on other faces. If you wish to manually make changes to the focus and exposure, do the following:

Tap the screen to display the AF area and exposure settings.
Touch where you want to move the focus area.
Drag the Adjust Exposure button up or down next to the focus area to adjust the exposure.
To lock the manual focus and exposure settings for future images, touch and hold the focus area until

the AE / AF lock appears; Tap the screen to unlock the settings.

Take low light images with night mode

On supported models, use night mode to capture more detail and brighten your photos in low-light conditions. The duration of exposure at night is determined automatically, but you can experiment with manual control.

The camera is in photo mode. The flash and night mode buttons are displayed in the upper left corner of the screen. The flash button is off and the night mode button is active. The Live Photo button is located in the upper right corner. The photo and video viewer is located in the lower-left corner. The shutter button is in the center of the center, and the camera select button is in the lower right corner.

Night mode is automatically switched on in low-light conditions. When the Night mode button at the top of the screen turns yellow, Night mode is on. A number appears next to the Night mode button to indicate how many seconds it will take the camera to shoot.

Press the shutter button, then hold the camera still to shoot. To experiment with night mode, press the night mode button, then use the slider under the frame to select automatic and maximum timers. Using Auto, the exposure time is known automatically; Max works with the longest exposure time.

Real-time photography

The Real-Time Photo feature captures what happens right before and after taking a photo, including sound.

- Select Photo mode.
- Click the Live Photo button to turn Live Photos on or off.
- Press the shutter button to shoot.
- You can edit Images directly in Photos. In your Live Photo album, 'Live' is marked in the corner.
- Take a selfie
- Use the front camera to take a selfie in Photo or Portrait mode (supported models).

Click the camera select button to go to the front camera. On iPhone SE (2nd generation), iPhone 11, iPhone 11 Pro, and iPhone 11 Pro Max, tap the Back button in the camera selection.

Hold your iPhone in front of you.

Advice. On the iPhone 11, iPhone 11 Pro, and iPhone 11 Pro Max, you can press the arrows inside the frame to enlarge the field of view.

Press the shutter button or any volume button to shoot.

Take a panoramic photo

Use the panorama mode to capture landscapes or other images that do not fit the camera screen.

Select the panorama mode, and then press the shutter button.

Slowly rotate in the direction of the arrow, keeping the arrow on the center line.

To finish, press the shutter button again.

Click the arrows to rotate them in the opposite direction. To rotate vertically, rotate iPhone to landscape orientation. You can also change the direction of the vertical pan.

Take a photo with a filter

Select a photo or portrait mode, and then click Filter. On iPhone SE (2nd generation), iPhone 11, iPhone 11 Pro, and iPhone 11 Pro Max, click Camera Control and then click Filter.

Under the preview screen, swipe left or right to preview them; Tap a friend to select it.
You can remove or change the photo filter in Photos.

Continuous shooting photography

Continuous shooting mode takes several high-speed photos, so you have many photos to choose from. You can take continuous photos with the rear and front cameras.

On iPhone SE (second generation), iPhone 11, iPhone 11 Pro, and iPhone 11 Pro Max swipe the shutter button on the left to take a picture. On all other models, press and hold the shutter button.

The counter shows how many pictures you have taken.

Raise your finger to stop.

To select the photos you want to save, tap the Batch thumbnail, and then tap Select.

Gray dots below the thumbnails indicate the suggested images to save.

Tap the circle in the lower right corner of each photo you want to save as each photo, and then tap Done.

To delete an entire series, tap the thumbnail, and then click Delete.

Record videos with your iPhone camera

Use the camera to record video on your iPhone and change the modes for slow-motion recording and video recording.

Make a movie

Select a video mode.

Press the Record button or any of the volume buttons to start recording. During recording, you can do the following:

Press the white shutter button to take photos.

Tap the screen to zoom in and out. To zoom in more accurately on models with dual and triple-camera systems, press and hold 1x, then drag the slider to the left. Press 1x to zoom out on iPhone 11; Tap .5 to zoom out on the iPhone 11 Pro and iPhone 11 Pro Max.

Press the Record button or any of the volume buttons to stop recording.

By default, video is recorded at 30 frames per second (frames. Depending on your model, you can select other resolution and frame rate settings from the Settings> Camera> Video recording menu. The faster the frame rate and the higher the resolution, the higher the recording video file.

On models with stereo recording, iPhone records your video in stereo by default. To turn off stereo recording, go to Settings> Camera and then turn off the stereo recording.

Get the language and region on iPhone

You set the language and region of the iPhone during the setup process. If you are traveling or moving, you can change the language or region.

Go to Settings> General> Language & Region.

Put it like this:

Language for iPhone

Area

Calendar format

Unit of temperature (degrees C or Fahrenheit)

To add a keyboard for another language, go to Settings> General> Keyboards> Keyboards, and then tap Add new keyboard.

Snap a screenshot or screen save to iPhone

Screenshot can be taken as soon as it appears, or make screen record to share with others or use in documents.

Do one of the following:

- On an iPhone with a Face ID: Press, then release the side button and the volume up button at the same time.
- On the iPhone with the Home button : Simultaneously press and release the Home

button and the side button or the Sleep / Wake button (depending on your model).
- Click the screenshot on the lower-left edge, then click Done.
- Select Save to Photo or Delete Screenshot.
- If you save a screenshot, you can view it in the Screenshot album in Photos or in the All Photos album if iCloud Photos is turned on in Settings> Photos.
- Advice . To quickly create a PDF of a web page, document, or email, take a screenshot, tap a thumbnail, and then tap Full Page.

Make screen records

You can create screen recordings and record sound on your iPhone.

Go to Settings> Control Center> Control Settings, and then click Paste next to Screen Capture.

Open Control Center, click the Screen Capture button, and then wait for a three-second countdown.

To stop recording, open the Control Center, tap the selected screen recording button or the red status bar at the top of the screen, and then tap Stop.

Scroll to Photos, and select an entry on the screen. Type and edit text

You can use the virtual keyboard to add and edit the text in iPhone applications.

Enter text using the virtual keyboard

In any program that allows you to edit text, open the on-screen keyboard by tapping the text box. Tap individual keys to type, or use QuickPath (not available in all languages) to enter a word by moving one character to another without lifting your finger. To finish the word, raise your finger. You can use any method when typing and even convert between sentences. (If you press the Delete key after entering a word, it deletes the whole word.)

The iPhone keyboard displays sliding from one key to another to enter.

Note: Swipe your finger across the text to see suggested options for the word you enter, instead of predictions for the next word.

As you type, you can do any of the following:

- Enter uppercase letters: Press Shift or tap the Shift key and swipe to the letter.
- Enable Caps Lock : Double-tap Shift.
- Quickly complete the sentence with dots and spaces: double-tap space.
- Enter numbers, punctuation marks, or symbols: Press a number key or a character key.
- Undo the last edit: Move left with 3 fingers.
- Repeat the last edit : Swipe three fingers to the right.
- Entering emoticons: Tap the next keyboard, the emoticon button, or the Next keyboard button to switch to the emoticon keyboard.
- Enter accented letters or other alternate characters: press and hold, and then swipe to select one of the options.

The display shows alternative characters for the 'e' key.

You can also dictate text or use the Magic Keyboard (available separately) to enter text.

Highlight and edit text

To insert, edit, or replace text, do any of the following:

- Navigate long documents: Touch and hold the right edge of the document, then drag the scroll wheel to position the text you want to change.
- Paste text: Click to place the insertion point where you want to paste the text. You can also precisely move the insertion point by dragging it. Then start importing.

The draft email shows the insertion point where the text will be inserted.

Choose a word: Double-click the word with one finger.

Choose a sentence: Tap the sentence three times with one finger.

Paragraph selection: press four times with one finger.

Select a block of text: Press and hold the first word in the block, then drag it to the last word.

After selecting the text you want to change, you can enter or tap the selected text to view the settings.

Cut: Click Cut or squeeze three fingers twice.

Copy: Tap Copy or join three fingers.

Insert: Tap Insert or spread with three fingers.

Replace: See the Proposed replacement text or ask Siri to suggest replacement text.

B / I / U: The selected text format.

Show More button: See Other options.

Move text

In the text editor, select the text you want to move.

The phrase is highlighted in a piece of text.

Touch and hold the highlighted text until it is raised, then drag it to another location in the application.

If you scroll the bottom or top of a long document, it scrolls automatically.

The selected phrase will be displayed by the user by pressing and holding.

If you change your mind about scrolling text, lift your finger before dragging or dragging text off the screen.

Set Typing settings

You can enable or disable typing features such as spell-checking and auto-correction. While entering text using the on-screen keyboard, tap and hold the next key on the keyboard emoticons or the keyboard toggle key, then tap Keyboard settings.

You can also go to Settings> General> Keyboards. In the list, turn special input features on or off.

Correct spelling

If you see a misspelled word underlined in red, you can correct it.

- Tap the underlined word to see the suggested changes.
- Tap a sentence to replace the underlined word.
- If the word you want is not displayed, enter edit.

Use AirDrop on iPhone to send items to devices near you

With AirDrop, you can wirelessly transfer photos, web pages, videos, locations, and lots more. to other neighboring devices and Macs (requires iOS 7, iPadOS 13, OS X 10.10 or later). AirDrop transmits information via Wi-Fi and Bluetooth - both must be turned on. To use AirDrop, you need to sign in with your Apple ID. The transmission is encrypted for security.

Send item using AirDrop

Open the item, then tap the 'Share', 'Share', 'AirDrop', 'More options' or other button that displays the app's sharing options.

Do one of the following:

Tap the AirDrop icon in the sharing options bar, then tap a neighboring AirDrop user's profile photo.

Advice . On iPhone 11, iPhone 11 Pro, or iPhone 11 Pro Max, point your iPhone toward iPhone 11, iPhone 11 Pro, or another iPhone 11 Pro Max, and then tap a user profile photo at the top of the screen.

Above the sharing options bar, select someone you know who has a device nearby that is available for AirDrop. Their profile photo is displayed with the AirDrop icon. If the person doesn't appear as a neighboring AirDrop user, ask them to open the Control Center on your iPhone, iPad, or iPod touch and allow AirDrop to receive items. To send it to someone on a Mac, ask to allow them to be detected in AirDrop in the Finder.

To send an item using a method other than AirDrop, select a method, such as Messaging or Mail, from the sharing settings bar (program-dependent options). Siri can also offer ways to share with people you know by showing their profile photos and sharing icons. You can also use AirDrop to securely share app and website passwords with iPhone, iPad, iPod touch, or Mac users.

Allow others to send items with AirDrop to your iPhone

Open Control Center, and then tap the AirDrop icon.

If you don't see the AirDrop icon, tap and hold the upper left group of controls.

Tap Contacts Only or People to choose who you want to receive items from.

You can accept or reject each request as it arrives. Set the screen time for yourself on iPhone

With Screen Time, you can set permissions and restrictions on the use of applications, schedule downtime, and more. You can change or disable any of these settings at any time.

You can block applications and notifications while using the device.

Go to Settings> Usage Time.
- Tap Turn on screen time, tap Continue, then tap This is my iPhone.
- Tap Idle, then turn on the delay time.

- Select 'Every day' or 'Set date', then set the start and end time.

Set App restrictions

You can set time limits for a category of apps (such as Games or social networks) and individual programs.

Go to Settings> Usage Time.

If you don't have Hours turned on, tap Turn on screen time, tap Continue, and then tap This is my iPhone.

Tap Application Restrictions and then Add Restrictions.

Select one or more app categories.

To set restrictions for individual programs, tap a category name to see all the programs in that category, then select the programs you want to restrict. If you select multiple categories or applications, the time limits you set will apply to all of them.
Click Next, and then set the time allowed.

To set the time of day, click the Set date, and then set a limit for specific days.

To set a limit for more programs or categories, click Select Program, and then repeat step 5.

When you have finished setting the limit, click Add to return to the Application Restriction screen.

To temporarily disable all application restrictions, tap Application Restrictions on the Application

Restrictions screen. To temporarily disable restrictions for a specific category, tap a category, and then tap Application restrictions. To remove restrictions for a category, tap a category, and then tap Remove restrictions.

Set contact limits

In iOS 13.3, iPadOS 13.3, and above, you can block incoming and outgoing contacts - including phone calls, FaceTime calls, and text messages - from certain contacts in iCloud, at any time, or over a while.

If you didn't turn on Contacts in iCloud, go to Settings> [your name]> iCloud, and then turn on Contacts.

Go to Settings> Usage Time.

If you don't have Hours turned on, tap Turn on screen time, tap Continue, and then tap This is my iPhone.

Tap Restrict connection, and then do any of the following:
Restrict contacts at any time : Tap On-screen, then select Contacts only, Contacts and groups with at least one contact, or All.

Restrict contacts during idle time : Tap During the idle time. This is where the setting you selected on the screen is set. You can change this setting to Specific Contacts.

If you select 'Specific contacts', click 'Select from my contacts' or 'Add new contact' to select the people you want to allow contact with during downtime.

If someone is currently blocked from contact restriction from trying to call you (by phone or FaceTime) or send you a message, they will not be communicated.

If you try to call or send a message to someone who is currently blocked by your contact restriction settings, their name or number will be displayed in red with an hourglass icon and your contact will not be executed. If the restriction is for downtime only, you will receive a time limit message. You can resume communication with the contact when the downtime is over.

To continue communicating with contacts blocked by your Restrict Contacts setting, change the settings by following the steps above.

Select the apps with no restrictions

You can specify which programs you want to use at any time (for example, in emergencies), even during downtime.

Go to Settings> Usage Time.

If you don't have Hours turned on, tap Turn on screen time, tap Continue, and then tap This is my iPhone.

Tap Always allowed, and then click the Add or Remove button next to the app to add or remove it from the Allowed apps list.

Set limits on content and privacy

You can block inappropriate content and set restrictions on iTunes Store and App Store purchases.

Go to Settings> Usage Time.

If you don't have Hours turned on, tap Turn on screen time, tap Continue, and then tap This is my iPhone.

Tap Content and privacy restrictions, turn on Content and privacy restrictions and then tap options to set content permissions for purchases in the iTunes Store and App Store. Application, content ratings, etc.

You can also set the required password before changing the settings.

Restore iPhone to factory settings

You can use your Mac or Windows PC to erase all data and settings from iPhone, restore iPhone to factory settings, and install the latest version of iOS.

Important: Restoring iPhone to factory settings will delete all data and settings. However, before the iPhone is erased, you have the option to back up your iPhone. If you're backing up, you can use it to restore data and settings on your iPhone or a new device.

Connect your iPhone to your computer via USB.

Do one of the following:

In the Finder sidebar on your Mac: Select your iPhone, click General at the top of the window, and then click Restore iPhone.

Note. To use Finder to restore iPhone to factory settings, you need macOS Catalina. For previous versions of macOS, use iTunes to restore iPhone.

In iTunes on a Windows PC: Click the iPhone button in the upper-left corner of the iTunes window, click Summary, and then click Restore iPhone.

Follow the instructions on the screen.

Set apps location access

With Location Services, you can select location-based applications such as reminders, maps, cameras, and wallets that can collect and use data that indicates your location. Your approximate location is determined using information about cellular network, Wi-Fi LAN (if Wi-Fi is enabled), Global Positioning System (GPS) (if available), and Bluetooth (if you have Bluetooth enabled). When an application uses Location Services, the Location Services icon appears in the status bar.

Enable location services

If you didn't turn on Location Services when you first set up your iPhone, go to Settings> Privacy> Location Services, and then turn on Location Services.

Disable location services

Go to Settings> Privacy> Location Services, and select one of the options to turn off Location Services for some or all applications or services.

If you turn off Location Services, you'll be prompted to turn it back on when the next application or service tries to use it.

Read the terms and privacy policy for third-party applications to understand how the program uses the data requested by the application.

Hide maps in location service alerts

By allowing the application to always use your location in the background, you can receive notifications when the application uses this information. (These notifications allow you to change permissions if you wish.) Map notifications show places you've recently visited.

To hide maps, go to Settings> Privacy> Location services> Location notifications, and turn off Show map in Location notifications.

When the installation is turned off, you continue to receive location notifications, but the map is not displayed.

Change the location service settings for system services

Some system services, such as location-based referrals and location-based advertising, use location services.

To view the status of each service, to enable or disable Location Services for each service, or to display Location Services icons in the status bar when system services are enabled at your location, go to Settings> Privacy> Location Services> System Services.

Delete important places

The Maps app keeps track of places you've recently visited, as well as when and how often you visit them. Maps use this information to provide you with personalized services, such as intelligent traffic routing. You can delete this information.

Note : Critical locations are encrypted through and cannot be read by Apple.

Go to Settings> Privacy> Location Services> System Services> Important Location.

Do one of the following:

- Delete a place: Tap the place, click Edit, and then click Delete.
- Delete all places: Tap Clear history. This action will delete all important places on any device that has the same Apple ID.

Set a password on iPhone

For better security, set an input password to unlock iPhone when you turn on or wake iPhone. Setting a password provides data protection that will encrypt iPhone data with 256-bit AES encryption. (Some programs may choose not to use data protection.)

Set or change the password

Go to Settings and do one of the following:

- On iPhone with face ID : Touch face ID and password.
- On iPhone, Home button: tap Touch ID and password.
- Tap Enable Password or Change Password.

To view password creation options, tap Password settings. The safest options are your own alphanumeric code and a special code.

After setting the password, you can unlock your iPhone using Face ID or Touch ID (depending on your model). However, for added security, you should always enter a password to unlock iPhone under the following conditions:

- You turn on or restart iPhone.
- You haven't unlocked your iPhone for over 48 hours.
- You haven't unlocked your iPhone with a password in the last 6.5 days, and you haven't unlocked it with Face ID or Touch ID in the last 4 hours.
- Your iPhone receives a remote lock command.

There are five failed attempts to unlock your iPhone with Face ID or Touch ID. Attempts have been made to use emergency SOS (see Making an emergency call on iPhone).

Attempts are being made to see your medical ID (see Creating and Providing a Health Certificate with iPhone Health Care).

Change when iPhone locks automatically

Go to Settings> Display and brightness> Auto-lock, and then set the length of time.

Delete data after 10 failed passwords

Set iPhone to erase all information, media, and personal settings after 10 consecutive failed password attempts.
Go to Settings and do one of the following:

- On iPhone with face ID: Touch face ID and password.
- On iPhone with Home button: Touch Touch ID and password.

Turn on Clear Data.

After all data has been erased, you must either restore the device from a backup or reset it as new.

Disable password

Go to Settings and do one of the following:

- On iPhone with face ID: Touch face ID and password.
- On iPhone with Home button: Touch Touch ID and password.
- Tap Disable password.

Set up Face ID on iPhone

Use Face ID (compatible models) to unlock your iPhone, verify purchases and payments, and log in to many third-party apps just by staring at your iPhone.

You must also set a password on your iPhone to use Face ID.

Set up a Face ID or add an alternate look

If you didn't set up Face ID when you first set up iPhone, go to Settings> Face ID & Passcode> Set up Face ID, and then follow the on-screen instructions. To set up an additional face ID look, go to Settings> Face ID and Password> Set Alternate Look, and follow the on-screen instructions.

If you have physical limitations, you can touch Availability settings when setting up Face ID. When you do this, the face recognition setting does not require full head movement. Using Face ID is still safe, but it requires more consistency in how you look at your iPhone. Face ID also has an accessibility feature that you can use if you are blind or visually impaired. If you don't want Face ID to ask you to open your eyes on your iPhone, go to Settings> Accessibility, and then turn off Face ID. This feature automatically shuts off if you turn on VoiceOver when you first set up iPhone.

Temporarily disable Face ID

Press and hold the side button and the volume button for 2 seconds.
When the sliders appear, press the side button to lock your iPhone immediately.

iPhone locks automatically if you don't touch the screen for a minute or longer.
The next time you unlock iPhone with your password, Face ID will be re-enabled.

Disable Face ID

Go to Settings> Face ID and Password.

Do one of the following:

- Disable Face ID for certain items only: Disable one or more options: unlock iPhone, Apple Pay, iTunes & App Store, or Safari AutoFill.
- Disabling Face ID: Click Reset Face ID.

Create website and app passwords on iPhone

By signing up for the service on websites and apps, you can allow iPhone to create strong passwords for your multiple accounts or create your own. iPhone saves passwords in iCloud Keychain and automatically fills them in for you, so you don't need to memorize them. If you use the same password in multiple accounts, iPhone marks it for you.

If you have physical limitations, you can touch Availability settings when setting up Face ID. When you do this, the face recognition setting does not require full head movement. Using Face ID is still safe, but it requires more consistency in how you look at your iPhone. Face ID also has an accessibility feature that you can use if you are blind or visually impaired. If you don't want Face ID to ask you to open your eyes on your iPhone, go to Settings> Accessibility, and then turn off Face ID. This feature automatically shuts off if you turn on VoiceOver when you first set up iPhone.

Create a password for the new account

On the new account or website screen, enter a new account name.

For supported websites and applications, iPhone will offer a strong and unique password.

Do one of the following:

- Choose a recommended password: Tap Use strong password.
- Create your own password: click Choose my password.

To later allow iPhone to automatically enter a password for you, click Yes when asked if you want to save it.

Automatically fill in saved passwords

On the login screen for a website or app, tap the account name field.

Do one of the following:

- Tap the suggested account at the bottom of the screen or at the top of the keyboard.
- Tap the AutoFill password button, click More passwords, and then tap an account.
- Password entered. To see the password, click the Show password text button.
- To enter an unsaved account or password, click the Keyboard button on the login screen.

View saved passwords

Ask Siri. Say something like, 'Show me my password.' Learn how to ask in Siri.

To see the password for your account, tap it.

You can also see your password without asking Siri. Do one these, then click an account to see its password:

- Go to Settings> Passwords and Accounts> Website and Application Passwords.
- On the login screen, tap the AutoFill Password button, and then tap More Passwords.

Weak password change

Go to Settings> Passwords and Accounts> Website and Application Passwords.
Weak passwords are indicated by a password reuse warning.

Touch any account marked with a multiple password warning.

A message explaining what makes the password weak.

Click Change Password, and then change your password on the website or in the application.

Browse web pages with Safari on iPhone

With Safari, you can browse web pages, add web pages to a reading list for later reading, and add page icons to the home screen for quick access. If you sign in to iCloud with the same Apple ID on all of your devices, you'll be able to see the pages you've opened on other devices and keep your bookmarks, history, and reading list up to date. Your devices.

A Safari window will open a web page with the address field at the top. At the bottom, from left to right, are the Back, Forward, Share, Bookmarks, and Page buttons.

Browse web pages with Safari

You can easily navigate the website with a few clicks.

Up : Double-tap the top of the screen to quickly return to the long top.

See more pages: Rotate iPhone to landscape orientation.

Refresh the page: Click the 'Reload' button next to the address in the search box.

Share link: Click the Share button.

Resize text, display and customize website

Use the View menu to increase or decrease the text size, switch to read mode, set privacy restrictions, and more.

To open the View menu, click Site Settings to the left of the search box, and then do any of the following:

- Resize a font : Press a large A to increase the font size, or a small A to decrease it.
- To view a webpage without ads or navigation menus: Tap Show Reader view (if available).
- Hide search box: Tap the Hide toolbar (tap the top of the screen to restore the box).
- To view the desktop version of the website: Tap Invite desktop website (if available).
- Install display and privacy controls for each visit to this website: Tap Website settings.

Website preview

Tap and hold a link in Safari to preview the link without opening the page. To open the link, tap the preview window or select another option.

To close the preview and remain on the current page, click anywhere outside the preview window. The overlay image shows a preview of the destination URL, then a list of possible actions: Open, Add to Reading List, Add to Photo, Copy, and Share. You can configure your settings in the Safari application to keep your browser private and protect you from malicious websites.

Manage your Safari privacy and security settings

Go to Settings> Safari, and then in the Privacy and Security section, turn any of the following on or off:

Prevent cross-site tracking: Safari restricts third-party cookies and data by default. Disable this option to allow tracking on multiple websites.

Block all cookies: Enable this option to prevent websites from adding cookies to your iPhone. (To delete cookies that already exist on iPhone, go to Settings> Safari> Clear

Warning for Fraudulent Site : Safari displays a warning if you are on a suspected phishing website. Disable this option if you do not want to receive phishing site alerts.

Apple Pay Verification: Sites that use Apple Pay can verify that Apple Pay is enabled on your device. Disable this option to prevent websites from checking to see if you have Apple Pay.

When you visit a dangerous website using Safari, a warning appears in the Safari search box.

Clear data and browsing history

Go to Settings> Safari> Clear Website History and Data.
Visit websites without creating stories
Click Pages, and then click Privacy.
When Private Browsing is turned on, Safari's background turns black instead of white, and the websites you visit don't appear in your iPhone's history or a list of tabs on other devices.

To hide websites and exit Private Browsing, tap Pages, then tap Private again. Web pages will reappear the next time you use Private View.

Conclusion

So, is it worth upgrading to the iPhone 11? If you've got an iPhone older than the XR and you're looking to upgrade, I think the answer is yes. The camera is substantially improved, and you will get vastly better battery life than anything aside from a XR. That's what most people care about, and Apple has really delivered here.

Printed in Great Britain
by Amazon